THE ART OF EFFECTIVE CONNECTION

Eight(8) ways to Unleash the Power of Association

By

Beau Parker

TABLE OF CONTENTS

Conclusion

INTRODUCTION

Welcome to a world where connections define our journey, where the tapestry of relationships weaves the fabric of our existence. "The Art of Connection" is an exploration into the labyrinth of associations that not only shape our destinies but illuminate the transformative prowess inherent in intentional relationships.

In an era where our lives are intricately intertwined with others, this book embarks on a journey to unravel the profound impact of associations on both the personal and professional dimensions of our existence. As we navigate the complexities of a social landscape, understanding the artistry of connection becomes paramount.

The pages that follow delve into the subtle nuances and dynamic interplay of relationships, shedding light on the hidden forces that mold our thoughts, actions, and aspirations. Prepare to embark on a voyage through the delicate dance of human connections, where each encounter, collaboration, and alliance contributes to the rich tapestry of our lives.

Join me as we explore the intricacies of this web, dissecting the threads that bind us to others and, in turn, shape our own narratives. "The Art of Connection" is not merely a guide; it is an invitation to reflect, learn, and ultimately harness the transformative power that intentional relationships hold.

Are you ready to embark on a journey that transcends the ordinary, unlocking the secrets of meaningful connections that have the potential to shape the course of your life? Let the exploration begin.

CHAPTER 1

THE FOUNDATION OF INFLUENCE

In the intricate tapestry of human existence, the people we choose to surround ourselves with serve as the foundation upon which our beliefs, behaviors, and aspirations are built.

This chapter delves into the profound impact of our associations, unraveling the intricate dance of influence that shapes the core of who we are.

The Foundation of Influence refers to the fundamental aspects that shape and determine the impact others have on our thoughts, behaviors, and aspirations.

In the context of human relationships, the foundation of influence encompasses various elements, including the people we surround ourselves with, the dynamics of social interactions, and the psychological mechanisms that underlie the way we are influenced by others.

Key components of the foundation of influence include:

1. Social Connections: The individuals we choose to associate with and the quality of these connections play a pivotal role in influencing our perspectives and decisions. Positive, supportive relationships often contribute to personal growth, while negative or toxic associations may hinder development.

2. Psychological Mechanisms: Understanding the psychological principles behind social influence is crucial. Concepts such as conformity, persuasion, and group dynamics shed light on how individuals are swayed by the thoughts and actions of those around them.

3. Identity Formation: Our sense of self is intricately linked to the people we interact with regularly. The foundation of influence explores how our identity is shaped through social interactions, including the impact of role models, mentors, and peers.

4. Intentional Relationships: Purposeful and intentional connections have a transformative effect. Being mindful of the relationships we cultivate allows us to steer our personal and professional development in a positive direction.

5. Personal Growth vs. Stagnation: Recognizing the potential for personal growth or stagnation within our social circles is crucial. Positive associations can serve as catalysts for development, while stagnant or negative connections may impede progress.

In essence, the foundation of influence is about acknowledging the profound role that relationships and social dynamics play in shaping who we are and who we become. By understanding these foundational elements, individuals can navigate their social landscapes with intention, harnessing the positive forces that contribute to personal and collective growth.

The Social Alchemy of Influence

This is a metaphorical expression that describes the transformative and often subtle process through which individuals are influenced by their social environment. This concept encapsulates the intricate dynamics at play when people interact with one another, emphasizing the profound impact that relationships and social connections can have on shaping thoughts, behaviors, and perspectives.

Key elements of the social alchemy of influence include:

1. Subtle Transformation: Like alchemy, which traditionally involves the transformation of base metals into gold, the social alchemy of influence refers to the subtle but significant changes that occur within individuals as a result of their social interactions. These changes may manifest in beliefs, attitudes, or behaviors.

2. Ripple Effect: Similar to the ripple effect of dropping a stone into water, the social alchemy of influence recognizes that every interaction creates a series of concentric effects. A single connection or idea can initiate a cascade of influence that extends beyond the immediate point of contact.

3. Unseen Forces: The term "alchemy" implies a certain mystique and hidden forces at work. In the social context, these unseen forces may include psychological processes like conformity, persuasion, and social norms, which subtly shape individuals within a social group.

4. Cultural and Social Transformation: The social alchemy of influence extends beyond individual interactions to contribute to broader cultural and societal transformations. Cultural shifts often result from the collective influence of individuals within a society.

5. Positive and Negative Transmutations: Influences within social circles can lead to positive transformations, such as personal growth, increased empathy, and shared accomplishments. Conversely, negative influences may lead to detrimental outcomes, such as conformity to harmful norms or the suppression of individual expression.

Understanding the social alchemy of influence prompts individuals to be mindful of the power dynamics within their social circles. It encourages an awareness of the transformative potential of interactions and highlights the responsibility individuals have in contributing to positive social dynamics and collective growth.

The Ripple Effect of Connections

This is a metaphorical concept that illustrates how a single action or influence can have far-reaching consequences, much like the ripples created when a stone is thrown into water. In the context of human relationships, particularly social interactions and connections, the ripple effect emphasizes the idea that the impact of our actions extends beyond the immediate moment or relationship.

Key elements of the ripple effect of connections include:

1. Concentric Circles of Influence: When a stone is thrown into a still pond, it creates concentric circles that expand outward. Similarly, in social dynamics, a single connection or influence can create a series of effects that reach beyond the initial interaction, affecting individuals and situations in concentric circles.

2. Amplification of Impact: The ripple effect suggests that the impact of a connection is not confined to the individuals directly involved but amplifies as it spreads. Positive or negative influences within a social network can influence the thoughts, behaviors, and attitudes of others in a cascading manner.

3. Interconnectedness: The concept underscores the interconnected nature of human relationships. Each person is connected to others, and the influence of one individual can reverberate through the network, creating a complex web of interdependencies.

4. Collective Consequences: Recognizing the ripple effect emphasizes the collective consequences of individual actions. Positive interactions contribute to a culture of support and growth, while negative influences can detrimentally affect the overall well-being of a social group.

5. Unpredictable Pathways: Much like ripples on water follow unpredictable pathways, the consequences of connections may not always unfold in a linear or foreseeable manner. The complexity of social dynamics means that the outcomes of influences can take unexpected turns.

Understanding the ripple effect of connections encourages individuals to be mindful of the impact they have within their social circles. It prompts consideration of the broader implications of one's actions, fostering a sense of responsibility and awareness of the interconnected nature of human relationships. This concept underscores the idea that small, intentional positive actions can contribute to a wave of positive change within a community or society.

The Science Behind Social Influence

"The Science Behind Social Influence" refers to the systematic study of the psychological and sociological mechanisms that govern how individuals are affected by the thoughts, behaviors, and attitudes of others within their social environment. This field of study explores the dynamics of social influence, shedding light on the underlying processes that shape human interactions and contribute to the formation of beliefs and behaviors.

Key components of the science behind social influence include:

1. Social Psychology Theories: Various social psychology theories provide frameworks for understanding how individuals are influenced by others. For example, theories on conformity (e.g., Asch's conformity experiments), obedience (e.g., Milgram's obedience studies), and social identity contribute to the understanding of social influence dynamics.

2. Group Dynamics: Social influence often occurs within group contexts. The science behind social influence examines how group dynamics, norms, and roles influence individual behavior. Concepts like groupthink and social loafing are examples of phenomena studied in this context.

3. Persuasion and Communication: The study of social influence includes the examination of persuasive techniques and communication strategies. Researchers explore how messages are crafted and delivered to influence attitudes and behaviors, encompassing factors like source credibility, message content, and audience characteristics.

4. Compliance and Authority: Understanding how individuals comply with requests or respond to authority figures is a crucial aspect of the science of social influence. The Milgram experiment, for instance, demonstrated the impact of authority on individuals' willingness to obey potentially harmful commands.

5. Norms and Socialization: Social influence is also shaped by societal norms and the process of socialization. The science behind social influence investigates how individuals internalize cultural norms and adopt behaviors that align with the values of their social groups.

6. Cultural and Cross-Cultural Influences: The impact of culture on social influence is explored to understand how cultural factors shape the way individuals respond to social cues and conform to societal expectations. Cross-cultural studies provide insights into variations in social influence across different cultural contexts.

7. Social Networks and Online Influence: With the rise of digital communication, the science behind social influence has expanded to include the study of how online interactions and social networks influence beliefs and behaviors. This includes research on social media, online communities, and virtual social dynamics.

By delving into the science behind social influence, researchers seek to unravel the intricacies of human behavior within social contexts. This knowledge has practical applications in fields such as marketing, public relations, leadership, and social policy, providing insights into how to effectively navigate and understand the complexities of social influence.

Catalysts for Personal Growth

Catalysts for Personal Growth are factors or elements that stimulate and facilitate an individual's development, leading to positive changes in various aspects of their life. These catalysts play a pivotal role in fostering personal growth by providing opportunities for learning, self-discovery, and transformation. In the context of social connections and relationships, several catalysts contribute to an environment conducive to personal development.

Key catalysts for personal growth within social connections include:

1. Supportive Relationships: Positive and supportive relationships act as catalysts for personal growth. Having individuals who believe in and encourage one's potential creates a nurturing environment for exploring new ideas, taking risks, and facing challenges.

2. Constructive Feedback: Honest and constructive feedback from peers, mentors, or friends can serve as a catalyst for self-improvement. Learning from feedback helps individuals identify areas for growth and development.

3. Shared Learning Experiences: Engaging in shared learning experiences with others fosters personal growth. Collaborative learning environments, whether formal or informal, provide opportunities for gaining new insights, skills, and perspectives.

4. Mentorship and Guidance: Having mentors or guides who share their experiences and insights can be a powerful catalyst for personal growth. Mentorship provides valuable guidance, advice, and a source of inspiration for those seeking to expand their horizons.

5. Challenging Opportunities: Opportunities that push individuals outside their comfort zones act as catalysts for personal growth. Overcoming challenges, taking on new responsibilities, and tackling unfamiliar tasks contribute to resilience and increased self-confidence.

6. Positive Role Models: Positive role models exemplify traits and behaviors that inspire personal growth. Observing and emulating individuals who have achieved success through dedication and hard work can motivate others to strive for their own personal development.

7. Cultivating a Growth Mindset: Encouraging a growth mindset within social connections promotes the belief that abilities and intelligence can be developed through effort and learning. Embracing challenges and viewing failures as opportunities for learning are essential aspects of a growth mindset.

8. Celebrating Achievements: Acknowledging and celebrating personal achievements, whether big or small, reinforces a positive mindset and encourages continued growth. Supportive social connections play a crucial role in recognizing and appreciating individual accomplishments.

9. Encouraging Self-Reflection: Social connections that foster an environment of self-reflection and introspection provide individuals with the opportunity to understand themselves better, identify goals, and work towards personal improvement.

Catalysts for personal growth within social connections are intertwined with the idea that meaningful relationships contribute not only to one's emotional well-being but also to their continuous development as individuals. By surrounding oneself with positive influences, challenges, and opportunities for learning, individuals can experience a transformative journey of personal growth.

The Perils of Stagnation

The Perils of Stagnation refer to the risks and negative consequences associated with a lack of growth, development, or progress in various aspects of life. Stagnation implies a state of inactivity, lack of change, or failure to advance, and it can have detrimental effects on personal, professional, and emotional well-being. In the context of social connections and relationships, experiencing stagnation within one's social circles can lead to several challenges.

Key perils of stagnation within social connections include:

1. Limited Personal Development: Stagnation within social circles may hinder opportunities for personal development and self-improvement. Without exposure to new ideas, perspectives, or challenges, individuals may find it difficult to expand their skills, knowledge, and experiences.

2. Lack of Inspiration: Positive social connections often serve as a source of inspiration. Stagnant relationships may lack the energy, motivation, or shared enthusiasm needed to inspire individuals to set and achieve new goals or pursue meaningful endeavors.

3. Negative Influence: Stagnant relationships can perpetuate negative habits, attitudes, or behaviors. Without the introduction of fresh perspectives or positive influences, individuals may find themselves caught in unproductive patterns that hinder their growth.

4. Emotional Disconnection: Stagnation can lead to emotional disconnection within relationships. Over time, if interactions become repetitive or lack depth, individuals may experience a sense of detachment or emotional distance from their social circles.

5. Diminished Creativity: Lack of stimulation and exposure to new ideas within stagnant relationships can result in diminished creativity. Collaborative and dynamic social connections often contribute to a more creative and innovative mindset.

6. Missed Opportunities: Stagnation may cause individuals to miss out on valuable opportunities for professional, personal, or social advancement. Dynamic networks are often catalysts for new opportunities, collaborations, and experiences.

7. Loss of Motivation: A lack of growth or progress within social connections can lead to a loss of motivation. When relationships fail to provide a sense of purpose or challenge, individuals may struggle to find reasons to strive for personal or collective improvement.

8. Strained Relationships: Stagnation can strain relationships as individuals may feel unfulfilled or dissatisfied within their social circles. A lack of shared goals, aspirations, or mutual support may lead to tension and conflict.

Recognizing the perils of stagnation within social connections highlights the importance of cultivating intentional and dynamic relationships. Actively seeking opportunities for growth, embracing change, and fostering an environment of continuous improvement contribute to healthier and more fulfilling social dynamics. Individuals are encouraged to be mindful of the potential consequences of stagnant relationships and take proactive steps to introduce positive change and vibrancy into their social circles.

Navigating the Web of Connections

Navigating the Web of Connections involves the strategic and intentional management of one's social relationships to foster positive outcomes, personal growth, and meaningful connections. It is about consciously engaging with and influencing the dynamics of the intricate network of relationships that make up an individual's social circle. Navigating this web requires thoughtful consideration of the types of connections, the quality of relationships, and the impact they can have on various aspects of life.

Key aspects of navigating the web of connections include:

1. Cultivating Intentional Relationships: Rather than relying on random or passive connections, individuals actively cultivate relationships that align with their values, goals, and aspirations. This involves seeking out individuals who contribute positively to personal and professional development.

2. Identifying Positive Influencers: Recognizing the individuals who serve as positive influencers within the social circle is crucial. These influencers may provide inspiration, guidance, or support, contributing to a more constructive and empowering environment.

3. Establishing Boundaries: Effective navigation involves setting boundaries within relationships to ensure a healthy balance. Clear communication and understanding of individual needs help prevent issues such as burnout or excessive emotional strain.

4. Networking with Purpose: Networking is approached with a purposeful mindset, focusing on quality over quantity. Building a network that consists of individuals with diverse skills, experiences, and perspectives enhances the potential for collaborative opportunities and growth.

5. Continuous Learning: Navigating the web of connections involves a commitment to continuous learning. Engaging with people who bring different perspectives challenges existing beliefs and encourages intellectual and personal growth.

6. Providing Value to Others: Building strong connections goes beyond personal gain; it involves providing value to others within the network. By contributing positively to the lives of others, individuals strengthen the fabric of their social connections.

7. Adapting to Change: The ability to adapt to changing circumstances within relationships is essential. Navigating the web of connections requires flexibility, as relationships evolve over time, and individuals may pursue different paths.

8. Investing in Relationships: Valuable connections are nurtured and maintained through active investment of time, effort, and care. Regular communication, mutual support, and shared experiences contribute to the strength of relationships.

9. Practicing Gratitude: Acknowledging and expressing gratitude for positive relationships enhances the overall quality of connections. Gratitude fosters a positive environment and strengthens the emotional bonds within the social web.

10. Being Mindful of Energy Exchanges: Recognizing the energy dynamics within relationships is important. Being mindful of how connections either contribute positively or drain energy helps individuals make informed decisions about the type of relationships to prioritize.

In essence, navigating the web of connections is a proactive and purpose-driven approach to managing one's social circles. By cultivating intentional relationships, individuals can create a supportive and dynamic network that fosters personal and collective growth. This process requires self-awareness, adaptability, and a commitment to fostering connections that contribute positively to various aspects of life.

CHAPTER 2

BUILDING A NETWORK WITH PURPOSE

In the vast landscape of professional and personal connections, we explores the transformative art of intentional networking. Here, we delve into the significance of building a network with purpose, understanding that strategic relationships have the potential to open doors to unforeseen opportunities. This chapter unveils practical tips and insights on cultivating a network that transcends the superficial, fostering meaningful collaborations and alliances that propel individuals toward their goals.

The Power Of Intentional Networking

Setting the Stage

In the world of networking, intentionality is the cornerstone of success. Before venturing into the realm of connections, individuals are encouraged to define their goals and objectives clearly. Whether aiming for career advancement, entrepreneurial ventures, or personal growth, a well-defined vision provides the compass for selecting connections strategically.

Identifying Key Stakeholders

Building a network with purpose involves identifying and engaging with key stakeholders. These may include mentors, industry leaders, peers, and experts whose experiences align with personal objectives. By actively seeking out these influencers, individuals can tap into a wealth of knowledge and insights that propel them forward.

Strategies for cultivating meaningful connections

1. Mutual Value Creation

A purposeful network thrives on the principle of mutual value creation. Successful networkers understand that meaningful connections are built on a foundation of reciprocity. Individuals actively seek opportunities to contribute, share insights, and provide assistance, creating an environment where both parties benefit.

2. Diverse Perspectives

Recognizing the power of diverse perspectives, intentional networkers purposefully cultivate connections with individuals from varied backgrounds and fields. This diversity not only enriches personal growth but also enhances problem-solving abilities through exposure to different viewpoints and approaches.

3. Effective Communication

The art of intentional networking involves mastering effective communication. Clear, transparent, and authentic communication builds trust and fosters strong relationships within the network. Whether through face-to-face interactions, virtual communication, or written correspondence, effective communication is the glue that binds purposeful connections.

4. Continuous Learning

A purposeful network is a dynamic source of continuous learning. Engaging with individuals who offer new insights and knowledge contributes to ongoing personal and professional development. The intentional networker remains curious, actively seeking opportunities for learning and growth within the interconnected web of relationships.

Practical Tips for Building a Purposeful Network

1. Strategic Networking Platforms

Selecting the right networking platforms is crucial. Intentional networkers strategically choose conferences, industry events, professional associations, and online forums that align with their goals. These platforms provide fertile ground for cultivating purposeful connections.

2. Investment of Time and Energy

Building a network with purpose is not a one-time effort but an ongoing investment of time and energy. Consistency in attending events, nurturing relationships, and staying connected contributes to the strength and vibrancy of the intentional network.

3. Adaptability

An intentional networker embraces adaptability. Recognizing that goals, industry trends, and personal development needs evolve, individuals adjust their networks to align with changing circumstances, ensuring continued relevance and effectiveness.

We concludes with the understanding that intentional networking is an art form, a dynamic process that requires vision, strategy, and commitment. By applying these principles, individuals navigate the intricate web of connections with purpose, unlocking the doors to opportunities and forging relationships that transcend the superficial. As we embark on this journey, the art of intentional networking becomes a powerful tool for achieving not just professional success, but a fulfilling and purpose-driven life.

CHAPTER 3

MENTORSHIP AND GUIDANCE

Mentorship and Guidance refer to the dynamic relationship where an experienced and knowledgeable individual, known as a mentor, provides support, advice, and insights to another person, known as a mentee. This connection is characterized by a shared goal of personal and professional development, with the mentor drawing upon their expertise to guide and empower the mentee on their journey.

Key elements of mentorship and guidance include:

1. Experience and Expertise: A mentor typically possesses a wealth of experience and expertise in a particular field or aspect of life. This knowledge becomes a valuable resource for the mentee seeking guidance and learning from someone who has navigated similar challenges.

2. Guidance and Support: The mentor serves as a guide, offering support and direction to the mentee.

This guidance can take various forms, such as providing advice on career decisions, sharing insights into personal development, or offering strategies for overcoming challenges.

3. Goal Alignment: Mentorship is often most effective when there is alignment between the mentor's experience and the goals of the mentee. This shared vision creates a meaningful connection where the mentor can provide targeted guidance to help the mentee achieve their objectives.

4. Skill Development: Mentors play a crucial role in the skill development of their mentees. Whether it's honing technical skills, leadership capabilities, or interpersonal abilities, mentors offer constructive feedback and suggestions for improvement.

5. Networking and Opportunities: Mentors often open doors to valuable networks and opportunities. Through their connections, mentors can provide introductions, recommend the mentee for opportunities, and offer insights into navigating professional or academic circles.

6. Emotional Support: Beyond professional guidance, mentorship often involves emotional support. Mentors provide encouragement during challenging times, act as sounding boards for ideas, and offer a perspective that comes from their own life experiences.

7. Mutual Learning: Mentorship is not a one-way street; it's a mutual learning experience. Mentors gain fresh perspectives from their mentees, and mentees benefit from the wisdom and insights of their mentors. This reciprocal relationship contributes to the richness of the mentorship dynamic.

8. Long-Term Relationship: Successful mentorship often evolves into a long-term relationship. While formal mentorship programs may have specific durations, the connections forged and the bond between mentor and mentee can extend far beyond initial expectations.

Overall, mentorship and guidance create a structured and supportive environment for personal and professional growth. The mentor provides a compass, helping the mentee navigate challenges, capitalize on opportunities, and develop into a more skilled and confident individual. This relationship is characterized by trust, open communication, and a shared commitment to the mentee's success.

Unveiling Stories of Mentorship

In the realm of mentorship, real-life narratives stand as compelling testaments to the transformative power that mentors wield. These stories illuminate the profound impact mentors can have on shaping destinies, influencing the trajectories of careers, and instigating personal growth. Let's delve into a few of these narratives to unveil the rich tapestry of mentorship in action:

Story 1: From Entrepreneurial Ambitions to Success

Meet Sarah, an aspiring entrepreneur with a vision but navigating the labyrinth of uncertainties that often accompanies the startup landscape. Sarah's story is one of entrepreneurial dreams ignited and realized through the guidance of a seasoned mentor. Her mentor, an industry veteran with a track record of building successful ventures, not only provided strategic advice but also became a source of inspiration during challenging times. The mentor's insights, drawn from years of experience, helped Sarah navigate pitfalls, make informed decisions, and ultimately turn her entrepreneurial ambitions into a thriving success.

Story 2: Navigating Career Transitions with a Mentor's Guidance

Consider James, a professional seeking to transition into a new career path fraught with unknowns and unfamiliar terrain. James found himself at a crossroads, unsure of the steps to take to make a seamless transition. Enter his mentor, a seasoned professional who had successfully navigated similar career shifts. The mentor became a guiding light, offering valuable insights, sharing personal experiences, and providing a roadmap for James to traverse the complexities of a career transition. With the mentor's guidance, James not only successfully transitioned but also flourished in his new professional domain.

Story 3: Shaping Leadership Excellence through Mentorship

Step into the corporate world, where Emily, a rising star within a large organization, aspired to ascend to a leadership role. The journey to leadership is often intricate, requiring a blend of skills, insights, and strategic thinking. Emily's mentor, a seasoned executive with a wealth of leadership experience, became her beacon. The mentor not only shared invaluable leadership principles but also provided constructive feedback, fostering Emily's growth as a leader. Under the mentor's tutelage, Emily not only ascended to a leadership position but also cultivated a leadership style that resonated with authenticity and effectiveness.

These real-life narratives showcase the diverse ways in which mentorship can shape and elevate individuals in their personal and professional pursuits. Whether navigating the entrepreneurial landscape, embarking on career transitions, or aspiring to leadership excellence, the impact of mentorship reverberates through these stories. It underscores the significance of seasoned individuals sharing their wisdom, experiences, and insights to guide and empower the next generation, creating a legacy of growth and success.

CHAPTER 4

COLLABORATIVE CREATIVITY

"Collaborative Creativity" refers to the dynamic and synergistic process where individuals with diverse skills, perspectives, and expertise come together to generate innovative ideas, solve complex problems, and create new solutions. It emphasizes the collective intelligence and combined strengths of a group, fostering an environment where collaboration sparks creativity and leads to outcomes that surpass what individuals might achieve in isolation.

Key elements of collaborative creativity include:

1. Diverse Perspectives: Collaborative creativity thrives on the diversity of participants. Individuals with varied backgrounds, experiences, and skills bring unique viewpoints to the table, enriching the creative process.

2. Interdisciplinary Collaboration: Breaking down disciplinary silos is a hallmark of collaborative creativity. Bringing together people from different fields or industries encourages the cross-pollination of ideas, leading to innovative solutions that draw on a range of expertise.

3. Open Communication: Effective collaboration requires open and transparent communication. Participants share ideas, feedback, and insights freely, creating an environment where everyone feels heard and valued.

4. Teamwork and Interdependence: Collaborative creativity is inherently a team effort. Team members rely on each other's strengths, skills, and contributions, fostering a sense of interdependence that propels the group toward collective goals.

5. Innovation and Problem-Solving: The primary goal of collaborative creativity is often innovation. Whether tackling complex problems or generating new ideas, the collaborative process is geared towards finding inventive solutions that go beyond what individual minds might conceive.

6. Adaptability and Flexibility: Successful collaborative creativity embraces adaptability. Participants are open to iterating on ideas, embracing feedback, and adapting to changing circumstances, creating a flexible and dynamic creative process.

7. Cross-Pollination of Ideas: In a collaborative creative environment, ideas are not confined to individual domains. Instead, they freely cross-pollinate, allowing concepts from one context to inspire breakthroughs in another.

8. Shared Vision and Goals: A sense of shared vision and common goals unifies collaborators. Whether working on a specific project or pursuing a broader mission, having a collective purpose enhances the cohesion and effectiveness of collaborative creativity.

Collaborative creativity can manifest in various contexts, including workplaces, educational settings, research and development initiatives, and creative industries.

It acknowledges that the collective synergy of a group often results in outcomes that are more imaginative, robust, and impactful than what individuals can achieve in isolation. Embracing collaborative creativity not only encourage innovation but also nurtures a culture of teamwork, mutual respect, and continuous learning.

CHAPTER 5

NAVIGATING CHALLENGES THROUGH COMMUNITY

"Navigating Challenges through Community" involves leveraging the collective strength, support, and resources of a community to overcome obstacles and address common challenges.

This approach recognizes the power of unity, shared efforts, and mutual assistance in finding solutions and building resilience in the face of difficulties.

Key aspects of navigating challenges through community include:

1. Shared Resources: Communities often pool together resources, whether they be financial, knowledge-based, or tangible assets, to address challenges collectively.

This shared resource pool enhances the capacity of the community to overcome obstacles.

2. Collective Problem-Solving: Communities foster a collaborative environment where individuals come together to identify and solve problems. The diversity of perspectives within a community can lead to innovative solutions that may not have been apparent to individuals working in isolation.

3. Mutual Support: Members of a community provide support to each other during challenging times. Emotional, social, and practical support from community members can be a powerful resource for individuals facing difficulties.

4. Knowledge Sharing: Communities serve as repositories of collective knowledge. Information and experiences shared within the community contribute to a collective wisdom that can guide members in navigating challenges more effectively.

5. Strength in Numbers: The sheer number of individuals within a community amplifies its impact. When facing common challenges, a united community can exert more influence, advocate for change, and implement solutions on a broader scale.

6. Networks and Connections: Communities offer valuable networks and connections. These networks can provide access to expertise, potential collaborations, and opportunities that individuals may not have on their own.

7. Resilience Building: Through shared experiences and joint efforts, communities can develop resilience. The ability to bounce back from challenges is strengthened when individuals know they are part of a supportive community that shares common goals and values.

8. Advocacy and Representation: Communities can advocate for the needs and concerns of their members, collectively addressing issues that impact the entire group. This collective voice enhances the community's ability to bring about positive change.

9. Cultural and Social Bonds: Beyond practical support, navigating challenges through community strengthens cultural and social bonds. Shared values and a sense of belonging contribute to a cohesive community that can face challenges with a unified front.

Examples of navigating challenges through community include grassroots movements addressing social issues, support networks for individuals facing similar health conditions, or collaborative efforts in response to environmental concerns. In essence, this approach recognizes that the combined efforts of a community create a robust and interconnected response to challenges, fostering a sense of shared responsibility and collective empowerment.

CHAPTER 6
TRANSFORMATIVE
LEADERSHIP

"Transformative Leadership" is a leadership style and approach that focuses on inspiring and motivating followers to achieve their full potential, both individually and collectively. Unlike traditional leadership styles that may emphasize maintaining the status quo or achieving specific goals, transformative leadership seeks to bring about significant positive change in individuals and organizations.

Key characteristics of transformative leadership include:

1. Visionary Outlook: Transformative leaders have a clear and compelling vision for the future. They inspire others by articulating a shared vision that goes beyond immediate objectives, encouraging a sense of purpose and direction.

2. Inspiration and Motivation: Transformative leaders inspire and motivate their followers to surpass their own expectations. They create a sense of enthusiasm and commitment by fostering a belief in the significance of individual contributions toward a larger purpose.

3. Intellectual Stimulation: Transformative leaders stimulate creativity and innovation by encouraging individuals to think critically and question the status quo. They promote an environment that values new ideas, diverse perspectives, and continuous learning.

4. Individualized Consideration: Transformative leaders pay attention to the individual needs, strengths, and aspirations of their followers. This personalized approach fosters a supportive and empowering environment where individuals can grow and excel.

5. Empowerment and Delegation: Transformative leaders empower others by delegating responsibilities and providing autonomy. This approach builds trust and confidence, allowing followers to take ownership of their roles and contribute to the overall success of the organization.

6. Ethical Leadership: Integrity and ethical behavior are central to transformative leadership. Leaders set high ethical standards, acting as role models for fairness, honesty, and accountability, thereby earning the trust and respect of their followers.

7. Cultural and Emotional Intelligence: Transformative leaders possess cultural and emotional intelligence, enabling them to understand and navigate diverse perspectives and emotions within the organization. This inclusivity contributes to a positive and harmonious work environment.

8. Continuous Improvement: Transformative leaders foster a culture of continuous improvement. They are open to feedback, embrace change, and encourage a mindset of learning and adaptation, driving the organization to evolve and excel over time.

9. Social Responsibility: Transformative leadership extends beyond organizational boundaries. Leaders with a transformative approach are often committed to social responsibility, seeking to make a positive impact on the community and the broader society.

10. Conflict Resolution: Transformative leaders address conflicts constructively, promoting open communication and collaboration. They view conflicts as opportunities for growth and learning, seeking resolutions that strengthen relationships and contribute to positive change.

Transformative leadership is often associated with positive organizational outcomes, employee satisfaction, and adaptability to change. By focusing on personal and collective growth, transformative leaders aim to create environments where individuals are inspired to reach their full potential, contributing to the overall success and evolution of the organization.

CHAPTER 7

CULTIVATING A POSITIVE ENVIRONMENT

"Cultivating a Positive Environment" refers to intentional efforts aimed at creating a workplace or community atmosphere that fosters well-being, collaboration, and a sense of belonging. It involves creating conditions that support the physical, mental, and emotional health of individuals, leading to increased motivation, productivity, and overall satisfaction. Cultivating a positive environment is essential for fostering creativity, resilience, and a positive organizational culture.

Key elements of cultivating a positive environment include:

1. Positive Leadership: Leadership plays a crucial role in setting the tone for the overall environment. Positive leaders inspire and motivate teams, communicate effectively, and lead by example, creating a foundation for a positive culture.

2. Open Communication: Encouraging open and transparent communication fosters trust and collaboration. In a positive environment, individuals feel comfortable expressing their ideas, concerns, and feedback, leading to stronger relationships and problem-solving.

3. Recognition and Appreciation: Acknowledging and appreciating the efforts and achievements of individuals is vital. Recognition creates a positive feedback loop, reinforcing positive behaviors and contributing to a culture of gratitude.

4. Inclusivity and Diversity: Valuing and celebrating diversity fosters a positive and inclusive environment. When individuals feel accepted and respected regardless of their background, they are more likely to contribute actively and feel a sense of belonging.

5. Work-Life Balance: Supporting work-life balance contributes to the overall well-being of individuals. Policies and practices that prioritize a healthy balance between work and personal life promote a positive environment by reducing stress and burnout.

6. Professional Development Opportunities: Providing opportunities for learning and growth demonstrates a commitment to individuals' development. In a positive environment, there is a focus on continuous improvement and supporting employees in reaching their full potential.

7. Empowerment and Autonomy: Cultivating a positive environment involves empowering individuals by providing them with autonomy and decision-making responsibilities. When individuals have a sense of control over their work, it enhances motivation and job satisfaction.

8. Wellness Programs: Implementing wellness initiatives, such as fitness programs, mental health support, and stress management resources, contributes to a positive environment by prioritizing the overall health and well-being of individuals.

9. Flexibility: Offering flexibility in work arrangements, such as remote work options or flexible schedules, supports a positive environment. Flexibility recognizes the diverse needs of individuals and promotes a healthy work-life balance.

10. Collaboration and Team Building: Encouraging collaboration and team-building activities fosters positive relationships among team members. Strong interpersonal connections contribute to a supportive and cohesive work environment.

Cultivating a positive environment is an ongoing process that requires a commitment from leadership and active participation from all members of the community or organization. The benefits extend beyond individual well-being to positively impact teamwork, innovation, and the overall success of the group.

CHAPTER 8

GLOBAL NETWORKS AND CULTURAL INTELLIGENCE

In our interconnected world, the ability to navigate global networks and demonstrate cultural intelligence has become increasingly crucial.

Globalization has blurred geographical boundaries, creating diverse networks where individuals and organizations collaborate across cultures. Cultural intelligence, or cultural quotient (CQ), is the capability to understand, communicate, and effectively interact with people from different cultural backgrounds.

Together, global networks and cultural intelligence play a pivotal role in fostering international collaboration, driving innovation, and building inclusive communities.

The Impact of Global Networks

1. Interconnected Economies: Global networks form the backbone of interconnected economies, facilitating international trade, investment, and economic collaboration. Businesses are now part of a global ecosystem where supply chains, markets, and resources span across continents.

2. Knowledge Exchange: Global networks serve as conduits for knowledge exchange. Researchers, scientists, and academics collaborate on a global scale, accelerating the pace of discovery and innovation in various fields.

3. Cross-Cultural Collaboration: Professionals engage in cross-cultural collaborations within global networks, bringing together diverse perspectives to solve complex problems. This collaboration fosters creativity and a rich exchange of ideas.

4. Diverse Talent Pool: Organizations tap into global networks to access a diverse talent pool. Virtual teams comprised of individuals from different countries contribute a variety of skills, experiences, and cultural insights, enriching the work environment.

5. International Diplomacy: 7Global networks are instrumental in international diplomacy. Governments, non-governmental organizations, and international bodies use these networks to address global challenges, negotiate treaties, and promote cooperation.

The Significance of Cultural Intelligence

1. Understanding Cultural Nuances: Cultural intelligence involves the ability to understand and navigate cultural nuances. This includes recognizing communication styles, customs, and social norms, which are crucial for effective cross-cultural interactions.

2. Adaptability: Individuals with high cultural intelligence demonstrate adaptability in diverse cultural settings. This adaptability extends to various contexts, such as business negotiations, diplomatic relations, or working within multicultural teams.

3. Effective Communication: Cultural intelligence enhances effective communication across cultures. It involves not only language proficiency but also an understanding of how communication preferences, non-verbal cues, and decision-making processes vary among cultures.

4. Respect and Inclusivity: Cultural intelligence fosters respect and inclusivity. Individuals who are culturally intelligent are mindful of cultural differences, avoiding stereotypes and biases, and promoting an inclusive and welcoming environment.

5. Conflict Resolution: Cultural intelligence plays a key role in conflict resolution. Understanding cultural factors that may contribute to conflicts helps individuals navigate disputes more effectively and find culturally sensitive resolutions.

Building Cultural Intelligence in Global Networks

1. Cross-Cultural Training: Offering cross-cultural training programs equips individuals with the knowledge and skills to navigate cultural differences effectively. This training may cover cultural awareness, communication strategies, and global etiquette.

2. Diverse Leadership: Promoting diverse leadership at all levels of an organization contributes to cultural intelligence. Diverse leadership brings varied perspectives to decision-making processes and sets an inclusive tone.

3. Cultural Exchanges: Encouraging cultural exchanges, whether through international assignments, virtual collaborations, or study programs, provides individuals with firsthand experiences that enhance cultural intelligence.

4. Continuous Learning: Cultural intelligence is a dynamic skill that requires continuous learning. Encouraging a culture of curiosity, openness, and ongoing education about different cultures contributes to building and maintaining high CQ.

5. Mentorship and Coaching: Mentorship and coaching programs that focus on cultural intelligence provide individuals with guidance and support as they navigate global networks. Experienced mentors can share insights and strategies for effective cross-cultural interactions.

The synergy between global networks and cultural intelligence is transformative in our interconnected world. Organizations and individuals that embrace this synergy are better positioned to thrive in diverse and dynamic global environments, fostering collaboration, understanding, and innovation across cultures.

CONCLUSION

"The Art of Effective Connection" concludes with a call to action, urging readers to reflect on their associations and take intentional steps towards building a network that empowers and uplifts. It asserts that the true power of association lies not only in individual success but in the collective elevation of humanity.

we find ourselves at the intersection of profound insights into the transformative power of connections and the visionary realm of transformative leadership. This journey has taken us through the intricate web of associations that shape our destinies and has unveiled the transformative potential of intentional relationships. As we reflect on the transformative leadership principles and the dynamics of collaborative creativity, mentorship, and global networks, it becomes clear that connection is not merely a transactional concept but a catalyst for growth, innovation, and positive change.

At the heart of transformative leadership lies the ability to inspire, empower, and elevate individuals towards a shared vision. It is a leadership style that transcends traditional models, embracing the principles of ethical conduct, cultural intelligence, and continuous improvement. As we've witnessed, transformative leaders are architects of change, cultivating positive environments where individuals thrive, contribute, and find purpose.

"The Art of Effective Connection" emphasizes that true leadership is not solitary; it is about fostering connections, both individual and collective, that create ripples of positive impact. We've explored the ripple effect of connections, witnessed the alchemy of influence, and navigated the challenges and triumphs of building networks with purpose. These principles underscore the importance of creating a culture of collaboration, inclusivity, and continuous learning within organizations and communities.

In the realm of mentorship, real-life narratives have unfolded, revealing the transformative power mentors hold in shaping destinies, guiding careers, and instigating personal growth. The unveiling of these stories serves as a testament to the profound impact mentorship has on individuals and underscores the responsibility we hold to pay forward the wisdom and support we receive.

Collaborative creativity has been examined as a force that sparks innovation through the synergy of diverse minds. We've explored case studies showcasing the power of collective intelligence, reinforcing the idea that the most impactful solutions arise when individuals with varied perspectives come together.

Our journey through global networks and cultural intelligence has underscored the interconnected nature of our world. The ability to navigate these networks with cultural sensitivity and intelligence has emerged as a critical skill for leaders in the 21st century, enabling them to foster inclusive environments, drive innovation, and contribute to global progress.

As we conclude this exploration, it is evident that "The Art of Effective Connection" is a dynamic tapestry woven with threads of intentional relationships, transformative leadership, and the collaborative spirit. It is a guide for leaders, aspiring leaders, and individuals seeking to harness the power of connections for positive change.

The essence of this book lies in the understanding that, at its core, leadership is a relational art, and the artful cultivation of these connections has the potential to transform not only individuals but the fabric of the organizations and communities they inhabit.

May the principles explored here serve as beacons, guiding us toward a future where connection, collaboration, and transformative leadership prevail, creating a tapestry of positive impact that transcends boundaries and inspires generations to come.